WORKBOOK 3

prepared for the course team by ross fergusson

This publication forms part of an Open University course DD100 *An Introduction to the Social Sciences: Understanding Social Change*. Details of this and other Open University courses can be obtained from the Call Centre, PO Box 724, The Open University, Milton Keynes MK7 6ZS, United Kingdom: tel. +44 (0)1908 653231, e-mail ces-gen@open.ac.uk

Alternatively, you may visit the Open University website at http://www.open.ac.uk where you can learn more about the wide range of courses and packs offered at all levels by The Open University.

To purchase this publication or other components of Open University courses, contact Open University Worldwide Ltd, The Berrill Building, Walton Hall, Milton Keynes MK7 6AA, United Kingdom: tel. +44 (0)1908 858785; fax +44 (0)1908 858787; e-mail ouwenq@open.ac.uk; website http://www.ouw.co.uk

The Open University
Walton Hall, Milton Keynes
MK7 6AA

First published 2000. Second edition 2001. Reprinted 2001, 2003

Edited, designed and typeset by The Open University.

Printed in the United Kingdom by The Bath Press, Bath.

ISBN 0 7492 7728 9

2.3

24058B/dd100wb3isbn0749277289i2.3

Contents

The DD100 course team

John Allen, *Senior Lecturer in Geography*

Penny Bennett, *Editor*

Pam Berry, *Compositor*

Simon Bromley, *Senior Lecturer in Government*

David Calderwood, *Project Controller*

Elizabeth Chaplin, *Tutor Panel*

Giles Clark, *Co-publishing Advisor*

Stephen Clift, *Editor*

Allan Cochrane, *Professor of Public Policy*

Lene Connolly, *Print Buying Controller*

Graham Dawson, *Lecturer in Economics*

Lesley Duguid, *Senior Course Co-ordination Secretary*

Ross Fergusson, *Staff Tutor in Social Policy (Region 02)*

Fran Ford, *Senior Course Co-ordination Secretary*

David Goldblatt, *Co-Course Team Chair, Lecturer in Government*

Jenny Gove, *Lecturer in Psychology*

Judith Greene, *Professor of Psychology*

Montserrat Guibernau, *Lecturer in Government*

Peter Hamilton, *Lecturer in Sociology*

Celia Hart, *Picture Researcher*

David Held, *Professor of Politics and Sociology*

Susan Himmelweit, *Senior Lecturer in Economics*

Steve Hinchliffe, *Lecturer in Geography*

Gordon Hughes, *Lecturer in Social Policy*

Christina Janoszka, *Course Manager*

Pat Jess, *Staff Tutor in Geography (Region 12)*

Bob Kelly, *Staff Tutor in Government (Region 06)*

Margaret Kiloh, *Staff Tutor in Applied Social Sciences (Region 13)*

Sylvia Lay-Flurrie, *Secretary*

Siân Lewis, *Graphic Designer*

Tony McGrew, *Professor of International Relations, University of Southampton*

Hugh Mackay, *Staff Tutor in Sociology (Region 10)*

Maureen Mackintosh, *Professor of Economics*

Eugene McLaughlin, *Senior Lecturer in Applied Social Science*

Andrew Metcalf, *Senior Producer, BBC*

Gerry Mooney, *Staff Tutor in Applied Social Sciences (Region 11)*

Ray Munns, *Graphic Artist*

Kathy Pain, *Staff Tutor in Geography (Region 02)*

Clive Pearson, *Tutor Panel*

Lynne Poole, *Tutor Panel*

Norma Sherratt, *Staff Tutor in Sociology (Region 03)*

Roberto Simonetti, *Lecturer in Economics*

Dick Skellington, *Project Officer*

Brenda Smith, *Staff Tutor in Psychology (Region 12)*

Mark Smith, *Lecturer in Social Sciences*

Grahame Thompson, *Professor of Political Economy*

Ken Thompson, *Professor of Sociology*

Stuart Watt, *Lecturer in Psychology/KMI*

Andy Whitehead, *Graphic Artist*

Kath Woodward, *Co-Course Team Chair, Staff Tutor in Sociology (Region 07)*

Chris Wooldridge, *Editor*

External Assessor

Nigel Thrift, *Professor of Geography, University of Bristol*

INTRODUCTION

Block overview

Welcome to Block 3. For the next five weeks you will be studying some key ideas about how people's lives are ordered through some of the main institutions of UK society, and the ways in which power works in and through those institutions. There will be a particular emphasis on social change, on how far change has brought uncertainty, and on the growing diversity of UK society. We will also be introducing you to clusters of ideas, beliefs and social values about how lives should be ordered – these are known as political ideologies. And we will be focusing on the importance of theories in creating knowledge in the social sciences.

We suggest you divide your time between the different parts of Block 3 roughly as shown in Figure 1. The recommended route through the block is shown in Figure 2.

Study week	Course material	Suggested study time
14	Workbook 3 and Book 3: Ordering Lives: Family, Work and Welfare Introduction Chapter 1 Audio-cassette 5, Side A and notes	11 hours 1 hour
15	Workbook and Chapter 2	12 hours
16	Workbook and Chapter 3	12 hours
17	Workbook and Chapter 4 Afterword Audio-cassette 5, Side B and notes TV 03 and notes	$9\frac{1}{2}$ hours 30 minutes 1 hour 1 hour
18	Revision week	
19	TMA 03	12 hours

FIGURE 1   Course materials for Block 3

FIGURE 2   Recommended study route for Block 3

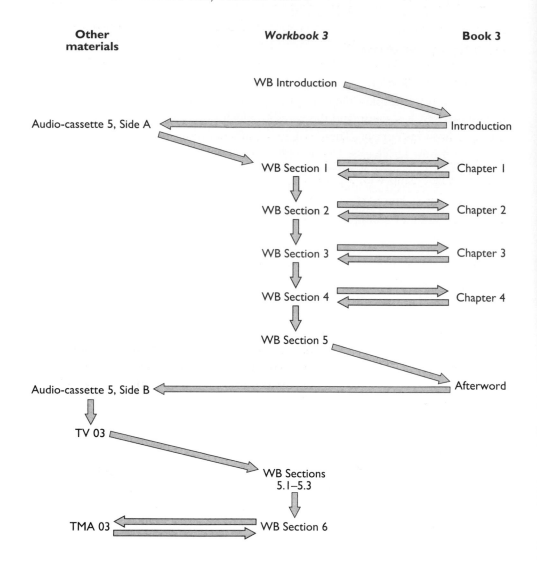

Key questions

How did you know what to do when you got up this morning?

Note down a brief list of what you did yesterday or today, and beside each activity put down a few key words which indicate why you did these things and what caused you to make these choices. (You will need to refer to your responses later.)

COMMENT

It would take us several pages to guess at the range of actions of individuals in a society as diverse as the UK. But if you look back over your list, we would be surprised if some of the following were not underlying influences which shaped your day:

- your need to earn a living
- obligations to dependants
- restrictions placed on you by lack of money or employment
- the requirements of an employer
- your relationship with a partner
- agreements with other members of your household
- the need to keep an appointment with someone in an official position.

It looks as though a great deal of 'ordering' is going on here. This might be ordering which we warmly welcome, because it makes us feel a sense of purpose, or belonging, or being cared about, or we might resent it because we would rather be doing something else. You might well have balked at our asking 'what caused you to make these choices' when tending the needs of an infirm parent, taking a reluctant toddler to school, awaiting a visit from a welfare officer, or being at work by 8 o'clock felt like anything but a choice. For less enjoyable activities, we mostly recognize that such things are part of the package of being a parent, or having a job.

WORKBOOK ACTIVITY 2

Go back to your list and your reasons for what you did. Make a note of how many of them are connected with families (yours or someone else's), with paid work, or with the welfare state. Then add a note on whether you are conscious of power being exercised, either through these institutions or from other sources, in shaping your activities.

COMMENT

It is quite likely that most of your waking hours can be accounted for by activities connected with families, work or the provision of welfare (by you or for you). Certainly, these are key institutions of UK society within which and through which many aspects of our lives are ordered. It would also be surprising if you were not sometimes aware of power being exercised. This might be quite overt, like your boss's power to make you arrive at work on time, or it might be power which works through your conscience, making you feel obliged to do something. Most of us recognize that our choices and actions are not entirely our own decisions for some or even most of the time. In other words we know that our lives are in some sense being ordered by forces outside of ourselves, however content or otherwise we might be with that.

The questions which drive Block 3 are about these processes. We will be asking:

- What are the processes of ordering by which society is held together?
- How do social institutions order lives?
- How does power work in and through institutions to order lives?
- How have political ideologies influenced changes in power and ordering?

Further questions then follow from these, which reflect the course themes. With regard to *uncertainty and diversity*, we will be asking:

- Are the ways in which lives are ordered through institutions changing?
- In what ways are changes creating uncertainty?
- Is power shifting as UK society becomes more diverse?
- Are changes in institutions reducing or increasing inequalities?

In connection with the theme of *structure and agency*, we will be asking:

- How far is power and order built into the structures and institutions of UK society?
- How far have active human agents brought about changes in the way our lives are ordered?

Key skills

Recognizing and using theories

The central social science skill we will be working on in Block 3 is that of recognizing and using theories. This builds on the key skills of constructing social science arguments and using evidence, which were the focus of Blocks 1 and 2, respectively. We will be thinking about how social scientists use theories to put together explanations, and the way theories work within the *circuit of knowledge* to put forward claims and to interpret evidence. In fact, theories play a critical part at every stage of the circuit (Figure 3). When we make claims, as a first step towards answering questions, we draw on theories, even if we are not aware of doing so. Evidence also requires a theory to interpret it. Facts do not speak for themselves: they need to be made sense of. And when we begin to evaluate claims and evidence we need to look at them critically.

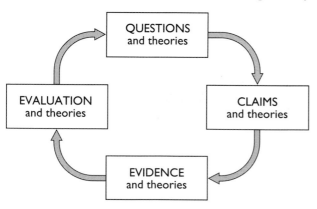

FIGURE 3   Theories in the circuit of knowledge

Revision and examination skills

The main study skill for this block is revising and preparing for examinations. This is intended to build directly on the reading and note-taking skills you developed in the *Introductory Workbook*, and on your work on writing skills in Blocks 1 and 2. DD100 does not have an examination, but we will be asking you to complete TMA 03, which is a timed TMA closely resembling an examination paper in its format and approach. This is intended to give you some first-hand experience of completing an examination, but with plenty of support and guidance beforehand, and full feedback afterwards, of a kind which you would not get in a 'real' examination.

As you progress through this workbook you will find 'revision skills', which are activities intended to help you to develop a wide range of revision skills and to help you practise some key skills of good exam-answering technique. Where there is a special emphasis on revision skills, these are shown by a 'revision skills' note in the margin. The main skills we cover are:

- active revision
- searching for relevant material
- assembling a story line
- summarizing the argument
- marshalling evidence
- writing practice answers
- actively searching for relevant material
- re-working lists/grids into an essay.

The final section of this workbook helps you bring these skills together, and gives further guidance on preparing for examinations in general and TMA 03 in particular.

It is quite possible that you will find some of the activities in this workbook slightly more demanding than for previous blocks. You should not be alarmed or deterred by this. In part it is because the key skills are more taxing than those for earlier parts of the course. It is also because we are deliberately increasing the 'gradient' slightly, so that by the time you have completed DD100 you will be well equipped to begin study at second level. Beginning to prepare for TMA 03 from the start of the block will also heighten the sense of extra demands. Our advice is simple: make sure you give yourself enough time to work on each section of the workbook after you finish each chapter.

Assessing Block 3

The assessment for this block is different from that for previous blocks in several ways. It will ask you to show an understanding of several parts of the block. You will have a fixed time of 90 minutes in which to complete it. And you will be required to do so without having access to your DD100 materials or any other notes or materials. We strongly recommend that you take this opportunity to complete this TMA in conditions like those which would be required for a 'real' examination by attending the timetabled session at your nearest study centre, if at all possible. If you have not already done so, ask your tutor-counsellor to confirm the date of the study centre sitting or, if that date is not possible for you, enquire at your Regional Centre about dates at other nearby study centres.

TMA 03 is intended to simulate some aspects of the experience of taking an examination. But in other respects, it will be very different. First, TMA 03 counts for only 16 per cent of your overall marks so your continued progress on the course does not depend on it. Second, you will have a copy of the questions well in advance of the cut-off date. Finally, you could fail or omit this TMA and still safely pass the course as a whole. Participation is not an absolute requirement, but we strongly advise you to make the most of this chance to 'get a feel' for exams, in preparation for your next OU course. We have therefore made this TMA non-substitutable – which means that you will lose marks but not be disqualified, if you do not take part.

TMA 03 will assess your understanding of the main topics of Block 3 as they are reflected in the key questions above, and assess your familiarity with the key skill of recognizing and using theories. There are two questions which cover different parts of Block 3. *It is therefore important that you study all the chapters and their associated workbook sections in Block 3.*

More details of TMA 03 are given in Section 6. Details of practical arrangements are included in the *Assignments Booklet.*

  Now read the Introduction to Book 3, *Ordering Lives: Family, Work and Welfare,* and listen to Side A of Audio-cassette 5 and read the associated notes. Then return to this point in the workbook.

1 POWER: ITS INSTITUTIONAL GUISES (AND DISGUISES)

Understanding how people's lives become ordered through social institutions requires an understanding of power. Creating order means fostering some kinds of actions and behaviours and discouraging others. The task of this chapter is to help you to think about how this is possible and the ways in which it occurs. This opens up fundamental questions about the free will of individuals, and the extent of human agency. How extensive are the powers of institutions? What are the structures through which they operate? As you can see, the DD100 theme of *structure and agency* is at the heart of this chapter.

Chapter 1 focuses on two theories of power. Both theories play a key role in the theoretical work of the chapters which follow, so it will be important to understand how theories are used to put together explanations and to see how these two theories can make sense of how power works through institutions.

You first came across the sociologist Max Weber in Chapter 3 of Book 1, where his theories of social class were contrasted to those of Marx. Closely associated with Weber's theories of class are his theories of power, particularly in relation to the form of social and political organization known as rational bureaucracy. To Weber, power can be seen in systems of rules, in identifiable structures, in the positions held by powerful people and groups, in their ability to control how resources are distributed, and so on. Insightful observation and analysis of the outward actions which occur in social institutions can tell us as social scientists what we need to know about who holds power, how it works, and how it is sometimes lost or gained. Watching the actions of key individuals and the events which take place within a government department, a board of directors, or even a hospital or a family reveals power at work, ready to be analysed and interpreted.

Michel Foucault's theory understands power as much less certain and predictable. How it works is less about things which can be seen like rules, or important offices of state, and more about prevailing understandings and assumptions about how to do things, and the processes by which these are translated into agreed actions. Power can move around between people and groups in sometimes quite unpredictable ways, partly because people are capable of rejecting dominant rules and fixed ways of doing things which they had previously accepted without question as the only way. For Foucault, internal processes and the interplay between people and groups is where power is exercised.

There are many other theories about power. We chose Weber's and
Foucault's theories for several reasons. They are both theories which were
developed specifically to explain how power works in and through social
institutions. The theories provide strongly contrasting views of power, and
very different methods are used to substantiate each theory. They therefore
exemplify very different ways of how social science knowledge is created. In
this sense they come from different 'traditions' in social science. Weber's
theory is long established and has exerted an exceptionally strong influence
over the social sciences. But it is a theory which some have thought less
adept at explaining how power changes hands, and how resistances to long-
standing structures of power sometimes succeed. Foucault's theory, in
contrast, is much more recent, is by no means as well established amongst
social scientists, is viewed with scepticism by some, and challenges some
accepted ways of producing knowledge in the social sciences. While it
seems better adapted to explaining how power moves around, its detractors
regard it as less clear about some of the most entrenched and resilient
workings of power, and how they came to determine the distributions of
power in the first place.

The two theorists also have significantly differing understandings of human
agency and how it shapes, or is shaped by, social structures, and more
generally very different approaches to understanding power. We will not be
concerned with which of them is more defensible and persuasive, but simply
with understanding what each approach can offer.

KEY TASKS

Chapter 1, 'Power: Its Institutional Guises (and Disguises)'.

- Develop a sense of the many different forms that power takes.

- Understand a range of different ways in which power
  operates.

- Recognize the need for theory in understanding power.

- Develop some knowledge of Weber's and Foucault's theories
  of power.

- Be aware of how power works within institutions.

- Understand the tensions between two different theories of
  power and the reasons for them.

- Practise active revision skills by compiling summaries.

Now please read Chapter 1, 'Power: Its Institutional Guises (and
Disguises)' and then return to this point in the workbook. You should
spend around two-thirds of your study time on the chapter and around
one-third on this section of the workbook.

1.1 Claims and theories: persuasion and domination

The chapter starts by asking *questions* about the safety of genetically-modified foods and, true to the *circuit of knowledge*, examines the contradictory *claims* about the potential harm they may cause and their benefits. But the larger question is about the relative power of firms which modify crops to secure their acceptance, irrespective of public preferences. Here, the competing claims are that the companies responsible might use techniques of persuasion or of domination to ensure that they can produce and sell such foods.

WORKBOOK ACTIVITY 1.1

Look back at how the claims about persuasion and domination are put together in Sections 3.1 and 3.2. How are they reasoned through? What prevents them going further?

COMMENT

The idea of the power of persuasion is based principally on the power of authorities, whose reassurances might once have been thought sufficient to declare these foods harmless. The reasoning is that firms use the power of expertise to allay concern.

The claim about domination is reasoned out by recognizing that it would be very difficult for Monsanto to dominate the food supply chain.

However, in both cases the argument stalls because it is not clear how far these modes of power are able to go. Is it enough to persuade people? Is it possible to force them?

What is missing is a theory of power to complete a reasoned account which amounts to an *explanation*.

WORKBOOK ACTIVITY 1.2

Make a note of how Foucault's theory would explain the claim that GM foods will become accepted by provocation. Then make a note to show how Weber's theory would explain that domination was necessary.

COMMENT

We have written our response in the form of a diagram of how theory works with the circuit of knowledge.

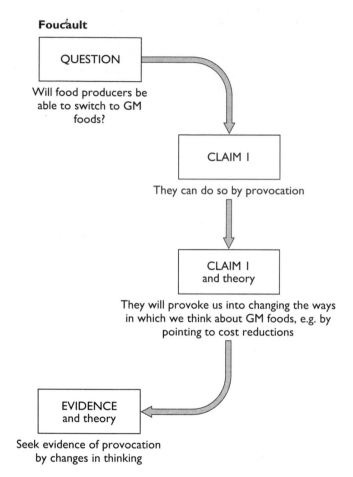

Foucault

QUESTION

Will food producers be able to switch to GM foods?

CLAIM 1

They can do so by provocation

CLAIM 1
and theory

They will provoke us into changing the ways in which we think about GM foods, e.g. by pointing to cost reductions

EVIDENCE
and theory

Seek evidence of provocation by changes in thinking

Weber

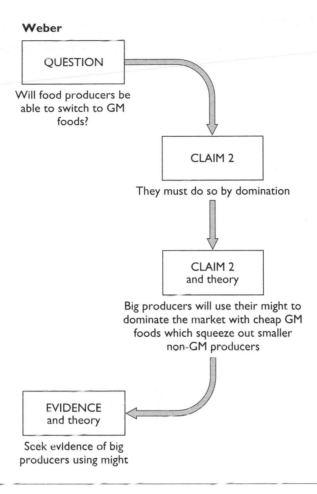

1.2 Evidence and theories: authority from above?

Section 5 put Weber's theory of power to work, thinking particularly about the evidence of how top-down power works in large organizations like firms and public institutions. The key concept here is rational bureaucracy – and most of us have direct experience of it. Here we want you to use that experience to test Weber's theory.

WORKBOOK ACTIVITY 1.3

Think about some recent encounters you have had with institutions and large organizations. Make notes which show how 'authority from above' was exercised. Check to see how far they match Weber's theory in Section 5.1. Make a note of any mismatches as well as similarities.

C O M M E N T _____

We would like you to assess for yourself whether your experience supports Weber's theory. Check to see whether it has the following features and how these relate to Weber's theory:

- special kinds of reasoning

- presumed authority of an official

- prescribed procedures

- 'standard' solutions/approaches

- reference to the rules, or a manager

- claims of impartial treatment.

Exceptions might include:

- adaptation when circumstances didn't fit rules and procedures

- secretive disregard for manager's view

- sense that the official acts independently of the organization.

1.3 Evidence and theories: governing the self?

Section 6 did the same for Foucault's theory. It clarifies its claims, and begins to look at evidence using the theory. The examples of the hospital patient and the university student, the household and the authoritative father figure are all ways of doing this. Again, the circuit of knowledge is clear: a *question* about power, some theorized *claims* from Foucault, an assessment of those claims with *evidence* interpreted with Foucault's theory.

We can work through this circuit for ourselves, beginning with the question: 'is there an anonymous "force" causing you, as a free agent, to act in ways which make it difficult to do otherwise?'

We should try to do what social scientists do when faced with such questions, and search for examples which support this proposition and examples which contest it.

WORKBOOK ACTIVITY 1.4

Go back to Workbook Activity 1 and look again at what you said about how you knew what to do when you got up today. Pick one example of something which you did more out of obligation than enthusiasm, then make some brief notes in answer to these questions:

- Could it be explained by what is expected?

- What are the 'ideas that go without saying' underlying it?

- Could you have 'done otherwise'?
- Are there 'anonymous forces' underlying this way of doing things?

Then check back to Section 6.1 and gauge how closely what has shaped your actions corresponds to Foucault's theory.

C O M M E N T _____

Again, we will not try to second-guess your answer. But see if you can find some of the following at work in your actions, all of which illustrate 'governing the self':

- avoiding conflict
- acceptance of responsibility in a 'role'
- respect for someone else's needs
- fear, shame, or guilt about the consequences of inaction
- desire to please someone you depend on
- your own or someone else's long-term interests
- acceptance without question or reflection.

Perhaps you found exceptions. If so, look back to the list of features under Weber's theory. How many of your exceptions suggest that your actions were driven by very real powers from external bodies: legal obligations, work commitments, regulations?

_____

Weber's theory is clearly concerned with hard-edged, clear structures which are entirely external to the person who is experiencing the power of rational bureaucracy. In contrast, Foucault's ways of 'governing the self' are much more about personal choices, individual decisions and the exertion of power from within. Characteristically, you may well have found that theorizing your questions using Weber put the stress on structures, whereas using Foucault indicates more scope for agency, albeit still heavily constrained by structures.

1.4 Active revision: structure and agency

The special timed TMA 03 is a month or so away, but in terms of the kinds of exam and revision practice it is designed to give you, a month is not too early to start. So this section is the first of several pieces of revision practice you will meet in this workbook.

One of the golden rules of preparing effectively for examinations is: **revise actively**.

Revision skills: active revision

Don't just read, especially don't just read a chapter from start to finish, and most of all don't read without a clear purpose. Search for something while you are reading: the answer to a question, relevant material to put into a practice essay, examples that illustrate this or contradict that. But search!

One good way of 'governing yourself' into searching actively is to put together lists, grids, diagrams and so on. We can try this out on what Weber's and Foucault's theories mean for agency and structure. It should get you looking back to the chapter and produce a useful summary of ideas distilled ready to be drawn on in TMA 03.

WORKBOOK ACTIVITY 1.5

Complete the first part of the grid below with short phrases which set out Weber's ideas about agency. This might take the form of concrete examples or generalized statements which could cover a range of examples, or both. Look back to the activities you have just completed and scan Section 5.1 for ideas. Then do the same for Foucault, using Section 6.1. Two or three points for each will be enough.

Agency	
Weber	
Foucault	

COMMENT

At the end of this workbook (p.69) we have completed the grid just with generalized statements.

- Check your examples and see if they fit our statements.
- See if your generalized statements and ours match.
- Find some other examples which fit our statements.

WORKBOOK ACTIVITY 1.6

What do these ideas imply for how the two theories see the place of structure? Chapter 1 says much less about this, but in the spirit of active revision, try to think through the respective importance Weber and Foucault attach to structure. Fill in the grid below using a mix of concrete examples and generalized statements.

	Structure
Weber	
Foucault	

COMMENT

Once again, use our completed grid (p.69) to check your responses and extend them.

End of revision skills

1.5 Power and institutions: ordering lives

The next three chapters in Book 3 are concerned with the institutions of the family, the employment market and the welfare state, and the ways in which they order people's lives. Each chapter uses Weber's and Foucault's theories of power to understand what kinds of ordering these institutions undertake. Chapter 1 has begun to show how the two theories work in institutions and what kinds of ordering they do. To practise active revision, we would like you to bring together what both theorists have to say about institutional power, think through your own examples of it and construct a summary.

WORKBOOK ACTIVITY 1.7

Read carefully through Sections 5 and 7 again and write down a few phrases about Weber's view of how power works in institutions and what kinds of ordering it is likely to result in. Against each one, make a note of an illustration of it from your own experience.

Repeat this using Sections 6 and 7 on Foucault's theory.

COMMENT

Here are two examples for each theory to illustrate what we mean. We hope you have found more, to enable you to do the next activity.

	View of institutional power/ordering	Illustration
Weber	Power is exercised visibly and people are told what to do	A complicated bureaucracy controls who is allowed to drive what kinds of vehicles
	Expertise puts professionals in authority to order lives	Social workers assess children 'at risk' and may remove them
Foucault	People become trapped in unquestioned institutional ways of doing things	In hospitals questioning, active people become passive obedient patients
	Expectations of how to behave in institutions are internalized by individuals	Teachers exploit pupils' sense of shame at 'untrustworthy' behaviour

We would like you to build on what you have done here, but also further refine your skills of preparing for examinations by summarizing some of the key features about the two theories of power.

WORKBOOK ACTIVITY 1.8

In two columns, list some of the key features of how power works according to Weber and Foucault. As you do so, try to bring out the contrast between the two by putting comparable points next to each other in the two columns. We have started the list below.

Weber	Foucault
<u>Who</u> holds power? Where power <u>is</u>	<u>How</u> does power work? Where power <u>circulates</u>

C O M M E N T _____

Check your version against ours at the end of the workbook (p.70).

_____

1.6 Modes of power and theories of power: the example of GM foods

We will now return to the case of GM foods and ask whether it represents persuasion, domination, or the exercise of authority. We can also consider whether the mode of power is closer to Weber's or to Foucault's conception. To remind yourself of how these three modes of power are understood by these two theorists, look back to Figure 1.8 in Chapter 1.

WORKBOOK ACTIVITY 1.9

Complete the grid below. You might want to do so solely on the basis of your reading of Chapter 1. Or you might feel able to bring in some developments since the chapter was written. (The examples we have given are, at least at the time of writing, entirely fictional.) You should do three things when completing the grid:

(a) *if you can,* provide a third example of your own for each of the modes of power,

(b) set out a brief theoretical explanation for the second example, and for your own example, and

(c) indicate whether the explanation is based on Weber's or Foucault's theory.

Don't spend too long on this: the key point is to be aware that there are some connections between these modes of power and theories, not to understand them in depth.

Mode of power		GM example	Theoretical explanation
Persuasion	1	Press campaign by supermarkets to claim benefits to consumer	Provoking a sympathetic response by appeal to self-interest of shoppers (Foucault)
	2	GM food chief challenges critical scientists to TV debate	
	3		
Authority	1	Ministers endorse continued GM trials and provide police protection full time	Use of formal visible power which ministers hold by virtue of their official position (Weber)
	2	Chief Medical Officer feeds GM meal to grandchildren	
	3		

Mode of power		GM example	Theoretical explanation
Domination	1	Suppliers of GM foods begin to withdraw non-GM alternatives gradually and without announcement	Constraints being imposed on consumers' choice by limiting options for those who refuse GM foods (Foucault)
	2	US dominance of World Trade Organization forces EU acceptance of GM imports	
	3		

1.7 Consolidating the key tasks

WORKBOOK ACTIVITY 1.10

Finally, before you move on to work on families, it would be a good idea to consolidate your week's work by returning to the list of key tasks with which this section of the workbook began, to satisfy yourself that you have something to say about them. If you have time, try writing a sentence or two about each. This will be a great help when you come to revise Block 3 in preparation for TMA 03, and at the end of this workbook we will suggest an exercise which builds on this work. If you find you cannot say something about each one, either try to make time to search a bit of the chapter which will help you with it, or make a note of what you think the problem is with a particular task and ask your tutor about it.

2 FAMILY: FROM TRADITION TO DIVERSITY?

Like the remaining chapters in this block, Chapter 2 is about how people's lives are ordered through social institutions – in this case, the family. It is also about how ordering reflects patterns of power. As you become absorbed in the material on the family, keep in mind the issues of power and order. They are what tie this block together.

You already know a great deal about ordering in families as a result of your own experiences, which we want you to use, but as a social scientist would – by treating them as evidence and by theorizing about them. Some of the social science you have already studied in DD100 is also relevant to studying families, particularly regarding gender, and we can begin by building on it.

WORKBOOK ACTIVITY 2.1

Note down quickly anything you can recall from Book I which might be relevant to understanding gender, power and change in families.

COMMENT

The discussion of changes affecting masculine identities in the first chapter of Book 1 raises questions about male economic power and gender roles in families.

Book 1, Chapter 2 on gender differences in identity raises questions about educational performance and men's and women's successes in the job market.

Chapter 3 of Book 1 looked at differences in earnings between men and women in different social classes.

As you read this chapter, keep in mind too the importance of theory. Weber's and Foucault's ideas about power will be used to think through the kinds of ordering which occurs in families.

Finally, this chapter introduces an important new facet of understanding the workings of power: political ideologies. Here you will be looking at the influences of conservatism and feminism as political ideologies in shaping the way ordering occurs in families.

KEY TASKS

Chapter 2, 'Family: From Tradition to Diversity?'

- Understand some important changes in families, particularly those which represent greater diversity and which have caused uncertainty.

- Think through some of the ways in which ordering occurs in families.

- Use the theories of Weber and Foucault to make sense of how power works in families.

- Look at how the political ideologies of conservatism and feminism argue for particular ways of ordering and distributions of power in families.

- Be aware of the place of social values in shaping political ideologies.

- Develop your techniques of searching for ideas and summarizing them for revision purposes.

Now please read Chapter 2, 'Family: From Tradition to Diversity?' and then return to this point in the workbook. You should spend around two-thirds of your time on the chapter and one-third on this section of the workbook.

2.1 Families!

It would be surprising if you read Chapter 2 without some reaction based on your own experience of families. Perhaps you found yourself in sharp disagreement with a point, relieved to discover that your experiences were not unique, angered by a particular set of values, or distressed about your future. The fact that the word 'families!' is sometimes used as an expletive says a lot about how emotionally charged the family is as a concept.

Such reactions are double-edged for you as a developing social scientist. They have potential to engage your interest and inspire you. Or they might distract you or cloud your judgement. We would like you to think about your reactions to the chapter, and make sure you can channel them to good effect. Since what we are doing here is social science rather than personal therapy, the most constructive approach is to acknowledge your own reactions, take account of them, and try to make active use of them.

WORKBOOK ACTIVITY 2.2

Take a light-hearted approach to what follows and don't agonize or spend too long on it. It is just for your own private use, as a check on your (and our) prejudices.

1   Imagine you are about to tell a close friend or relative about Chapter 2, to try to inspire them, or get off your chest something which annoyed you. Write a sentence about each of two or three things which inspired or annoyed you.

2   Now imagine explaining to a complete stranger what you mean by each sentence and why these points provoked this reaction in you. Try to articulate what lies at the heart of your reactions, giving particular attention to *social values* in shaping them.

3   Leave your notes to one side, then try to look on them later as 'data' written by someone else. Try to detach yourself from your own reactions. Rewrite those sentences in the third person, as though you were writing *about* a stranger. ('Jo's view is that ...', etc.)

4   Now try to stand your values on their head for long enough to be able to feel what it would be like to see the world completely differently. Make a note of what your (inverted) values now look like.

5   Lastly, ask yourself how social values fit the circuit of knowledge. Write a sentence or two about this or redraw the circuit diagram to give values a place.

COMMENT

If you have worked through this activity carefully:

- you will know enough about your own points of sensitivity to monitor yourself when issues arise on which your feelings will influence your thinking

- you will have begun to use your experiences in a channelled way as a source of illustration

- you will be aware of the part played by social values in your reactions

- you will have begun to envisage alternative ways of seeing and interpreting ordering in families.

What about social values and the circuit of knowledge? Our sentence reads like this:

Social values are almost always present in some degree in putting together explanations in social science, and they can affect any of the processes of producing knowledge by shaping what questions social scientists ask, what claims they make, or the kinds of evidence they collect or overlook.

We would represent this on the circuit of knowledge diagram as follows:

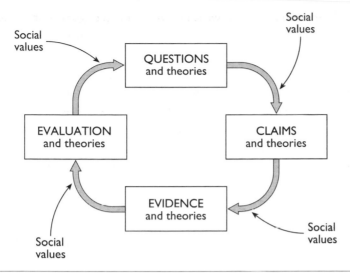

This, of course, does not mean that social scientists are helpless victims of their own values, still less that they indulge themselves by deliberately slanting their work to match their values. Most social scientists would claim either to endeavour to minimize the influence of values on their work, or to be explicit about the values which underpin their thinking. Very few social scientists would claim that there can be value-free social science, but there is much dispute about the degree of influence values can be allowed to exert and about the legitimacy of taking deliberately value-inflected approaches.

2.2 Searching for relevant material: ordering family lives

Imagine that you have decided to practise preparing an answer to a question in an exam such as:

What does it mean to say that families order people's lives?

How would you go about looking back over the work you had done to gather some relevant thoughts and ideas?

The key is to develop the skill of looking through the text quickly, that is: **searching for relevant material**. This involves the skills of scanning (introduced in the *Introductory Workbook*). In effect you will be spotting words and phrases which are flags that something relevant might be around. Think of it like flying low over a big city just looking out for one thing – roof gardens, for example.

Revision skills: searching for relevant material

WORKBOOK ACTIVITY 2.3

Search Section 2 of Chapter 2 for anything that is relevant to the question. If you are finding nothing, start looking for other flags.

COMMENT

On our first scanning, we didn't find much. The words 'order' and 'ordering' only cropped up a few times. Then we realized we were doing the equivalent of looking for trees and shrubs, when roof gardens are sometimes also made up of deck chairs and swimming pools. In fact, a lot of the material about traditional forms and contemporary trends in the family is really about ordering. Our notes read like this:

Traditional family
- mothers serve husbands' and children's domestic needs
- activity is ordered by roles, in partnership
- fathers 'in authority' literally order mothers/children

Contemporary trends
- gender no longer always basis of ordering
- order determined by marriage bonds less common
- women as employees and housewives: more money, less time
- divorce as breakdown in ordering of families?
- complex new ordering of 'multiple' families

Hidden amongst the descriptions and the statistics was quite a lot of potentially relevant material. The task now is to turn it into an answer to the question. This means using the notes as a prompt for ideas. They have to be re-worked to apply them to the question. Some will fit, others we will dump.

WORKBOOK ACTIVITY 2.4

Using *our* notes, put together a short paragraph which answers the question.

COMMENT

Leave aside your answer for a few minutes, and imagine that you are now the examiner. Read it over to see if it:

- recognizes that ordering is partly about organizing things to a pattern
- notes the place of gender in making that pattern
- sees that the idea of roles is about assigning people a set of behaviours/ actions

- refers to imposed order of an authority figure
- mentions making and breaking of contracts as a way of ordering/losing order
- recognizes that ordering can take multiple forms.

Your piece may not have used these words but will probably have drawn on these ideas in other ways. If not, go back to our two lists of features of traditional families and contemporary trends and think through how we got to these ideas from there.

So remember this sequence for revision and practising exam answers:

- read or invent a question
- scan
- make notes
- re-work raw materials into your own prose
- go back and check the finished piece to see if it answers the question.   End of revision skills

2.3 Counting families

Chapter 2 asked you to look through some quantitative data. You may have been tempted at points to skip over the tables and figures and just read what the authors thought were the important points. But some of the tables tell you far more about changes in the family than the few sentences in the commentary. You do need to get to grips with basic quantitative data for later courses, so here we are going to re-examine one of the tables.

WORKBOOK ACTIVITY 2.5

Reproduced here as Table 1 is Table 2.1 from Chapter 2 on type of households.

How has the left-hand column been organized? What can we deduce from the 'all households' data?

TABLE 1 Households by type of household and family, Great Britain

	Percentages				
	1961	1971	1981	1991	1998
One person					
Under pensionable age	4	6	8	11	14
Over pensionable age	7	12	14	16	14
Two or more unrelated adults	5	4	5	3	3
Single family households[a]					
Couple					
No children	26	27	26	28	28
1–2 dependent children	30	26	25	20	19
3 or more dependent children	8	9	6	5	4
Non-dependent children only	10	8	8	8	7
Lone parent					
Dependent children	2	3	5	6	7
Non-dependent children only	4	4	4	4	3
Multi-family households	3	1	1	1	1
All households (millions) (=100%)	16.3	18.6	20.2	22.4	23.6

[a] The term 'single family households' is used to distinguish them from households which consist of more than one family. A 'single family household' may mean a couple, or a lone parent.
Source: *Social Trends*, 1999, p.42

C O M M E N T

The table has been put together in order of increasing complexity of family type, from one-person households at the top to multi-family households at the bottom. Then most of the main categories are subdivided to give more detail about different compositions of households.

In addition, the table includes a row which says 'all households', showing that this is both 100 per cent and counted in millions. You might have been puzzled as to how it could be both. A very quick glance at the numbers in the column for each year shows that the figure at the bottom is not the total of all the figures above. The figures in the bottom row say how many million households there were in each year. Between 1961 and 1998 the number of households increased from 16.3 million to 23.6 million – an increase of almost 50 per cent. Also, you might have added up the year columns and found that (despite the note under 'all households') the percentages in each column don't add up to exactly 100. This is because most original statistical data give information to one or more decimal points. Social scientists often simplify this by 'rounding' the number up (or down) to the nearest whole number for the sake of convenience.

On first sight that seems unremarkable: presumably the population increased, but a moment's thought says that it is unlikely to have increased by almost a half. (In fact it barely increased at all over this period.) There are almost half as many households again in 1998 as there were in 1961. Size of households has, therefore, got progressively smaller since 1961.

The next step is to look at the trends of each type of household: are there more or less of each over this period? And are the numbers growing or declining disproportionately compared to the trends for other categories of household?

WORKBOOK ACTIVITY 2.6

Look at the trends for each category of household and note the biggest *proportionate* changes.

COMMENT

The big changes are that one-person households have become steadily much more numerous, single family households of a couple with 1–2 dependent children much less so. Lone-parent families with dependent children have grown in number and the other main categories of household have declined. But you will have noticed the word 'proportionate' in the activity. The change from 30 per cent of households comprising 1–2 dependent children in 1961 to 19 per cent in 1998 is obviously striking. But it is not nearly as large a *proportionate* change as the increase in one-person households comprising people under pensionable age, which are more than three times as numerous in 1998 as in 1961. And the increase in the proportion of lone-parent households with dependent children has been as dramatic.

So one of the most striking trends is that there has been a very sharp rate of increase in adults choosing not to live with other adults in households. This, of course, largely accounts for the declining size of households. Traditional family life understood as living with another adult (with or without dependent children) is very much less popular.

2.4　Family values: political ideologies and the circuit of knowledge

As we saw earlier, social values can shape any of the processes in the circuit of knowledge. There are few social institutions which are more subject to the influence of political ideologies and, hence, the social values upon which they are founded, than the family. The extracts from the journalist Melanie Phillips and Professor of Women's Studies, Lynne Segal in Chapter 2 illustrate this well. We would like you to use these to look more closely at how values shape ideologies. Several other political ideologies have plenty to say about the family but we chose to concentrate on conservatism and feminism here because they both see the family as central to how people's lives are ordered and because they take such starkly opposing views of how the social world should be ordered.

WORKBOOK ACTIVITY 2.7

Do an intensive 'analytical' reading of the Phillips extract (Section 3.1, 'Death of the Dad') and make a note of specific examples of conservative social values and the influence they have exerted over the questions Phillips asks, the claims she makes and the evidence she uses.

COMMENT

We concentrated on the statements that men's paid employment is important to 'cement masculine identity and to civilise male aggression' and that 'Britain faces a growing crisis among men'. Underlying this is the prevailing conservative premise that societies tend towards chaos as individuals pursue their own selfish ends. It is taken as read that men are inherently aggressive and that their aggression needs to be managed by occupying them usefully. The key value here is that of securing stability and maintaining order.

How has this shaped Phillips' thinking in the way she has tried to produce knowledge?

The extract does not actually include any *questions*. But all social science enquiry has questions behind it, even if they are not articulated. In this case the silent question seems to be: 'why is the social ordering undertaken by the family not working?'

This in itself bears the marks of values about stability and order. The idea that the processes of ordering are not working both implies that all was well in the past (a 'golden age' view) and that the present situation is a departure from it. Of course, both are highly questionable.

Phillips' *claims* are also heavily inflected by these values. The claims of male aggression are contentious, and reveal anxiety about a drift to disorder. Similarly the alleged 'growing crisis among men' is constructed from arguments about unemployment and lone parenthood which see these as symptomatic of disorder, rather than as functions of technological change, economic cycles or active choices by some men.

Inevitably, these value-driven assumptions are then mirrored in the *evidence* which is sought. Any change in male behaviour is assumed to be connected to 'the crisis'. The connection between these trends and boys' underachievement or the existence of men's groups are taken as read, despite being open to many other interpretations.

The point here is not whether the claims of conservative commentators like Phillips can be defended or whether the evidence for them is in fact evidence at all. It is that the way in which arguments are made and knowledge is produced cannot be understood in isolation from political ideologies and their values.

WORKBOOK ACTIVITY 2.8

Now repeat this exercise for the Segal reading (Reading 2.1). Take a 'sceptical' stance: you are looking for the ways in which she slants her questions, her claims, or the evidence she uses to endorse the values which underpin feminism. What are her assumptions? Note too where you are struck by the contrast between feminist values and conservative values.

COMMENT

We hope you have been able to find similar examples of feminist values and their influence over the way the argument is constructed by Segal. The contrast with the approach of conservatism is very clear, particularly in terms of social values. If possible, you might like to discuss this activity, particularly the contrast in values, with other students.

2.5 Feminism: political ideology, theory and social movement

You may have noticed the comment in Chapter 2 that feminism is an academic approach and a movement (often referred to as a social movement), as well as a political ideology. This is an important distinction in the social sciences. *Political ideologies* are coherent clusters of understandings about social structures and institutions which concern how power works in and through them. It will be clear that feminism conforms well to this definition: it is an argued-out set of understandings.

Chapter 1 says that *theories* are reasoned explanations which make sense of the social world. What distinguishes a theory? One characteristic is that it covers a range of situations and can normally be *generalized* as an explanation. So, for example, Weber's theory of power did not work just for thinking about patriarchal power but also for investigating the introduction of genetically-modified foods.

The term *social movement* refers to collective action by a group of people to bring about a specific social change. Social movements may be quite narrow in their intention, for example to prevent road building or nuclear arms proliferation, or they might be very broad, such as movements to secure equal rights and positive discrimination for people with disabilities. Feminism is a very broad movement, covering action which ranges from campaigns to secure equal pay in specific industries to long-running efforts to widen understanding of the oppression of women.

If we set theories, ideologies and social movements alongside each other, the distinction between the three becomes much clearer. We could summarize this as follows, using illustrations from three different versions of feminism.

Theories ...	explain the world as it exists now and how power is distributed in it.	Marxist feminism explains capitalism's dependence on women's unpaid social and biological reproduction of the workforce as a key source of women's lack of power.
Ideologies draw on theories to ...	construct coherent programmes about how the world should be, and how power ought to be distributed in it.	Liberal feminism draws up an argued case for women to have equal opportunities to men and equal social and political rights, to compete for jobs and other positions; justified by reference to liberal political and economic theories.
Social movements arise from ideologies to ...	secure social change, from the world as it exists now to the world as it should be by means of a transfer of power.	Radical feminism has mobilized women's groups to confront violence against women, by demanding police intervention in domestic violence, winning resources to fund secure accommodation, and exposing hidden violence.

2.6 Power in families: Weber's theory of patriarchal power

Weber's theory of patriarchal power is closely linked to his wider theory of
bureaucratic power but has two important differences. First, the personal
authority of the father figure replaces the authority which comes from holding
a particular position in an organization. Second, the father's power to
dominate depends on a tradition of duty and obedience from wife and
children, not on explicit rules based on rational order. What evidence from
Chapter 2 (and from your own experience) would support or query Weber's
theory? How well does it stand up to the changes described in Section 5? Can
we explain the emergence of feminism as a social movement from within a
Weberian perspective?

WORKBOOK ACTIVITY 2.9

We can use two key questions about who holds power in families, and who
makes rules about families, to explore further our understanding of Weber's
theory of patriarchal power. This involves following the circuit of knowledge by
asking a theorized question, making a theoretical claim, and using evidence in a
theorized way to try to answer the question.

Starting from the grid in Table 2.5 of Chapter 2 answer the following questions:

1 What are the theoretical claims regarding who holds power and who makes
   rules?

2 What evidence is there in the chapter as a whole to support these claims?

3 What evidence from the chapter queries these claims?

4 How far does the evidence suggest structures are stronger influences here,
   and how far agency?

COMMENT

1 Male power based on tradition is partly hierarchical as a result of superior
   male economic power.

2 Many women depend on men for money for their own and their
   children's welfare. Possibilities for asserting own will are limited.

3 As many women as men now have paid employment, albeit on lower
   average pay.

4 Men's economic power was based on their position in structure of work,
   but women have used their powers as active agents to grasp work
   opportunities which give some independence.

2.7 Power in families: Foucault's theory

Foucault's theory is much less concerned with visible, hard-edged power, and much more with its internalization, how it circulates, how it is negotiated and how it is contested. On this account, it is much easier to see how challenges to patriarchal power arose through feminism, for example. What is less clear is how male power became so firmly consolidated in the first place. Keep this underlying question in mind as you do the following activity.

WORKBOOK ACTIVITY 2.10

Answer the same four questions as before for Foucault's theory.

1   What are the theoretical claims regarding how power is exercised and how power circulates?

2   What evidence is there in the chapter as a whole to support these claims?

3   What evidence from the chapter queries these claims?

4   How far does the evidence suggest structures are stronger influences here, and how far agency?

COMMENT

1   Women and children in families may 'order' themselves rather than being coerced.

2   In many families there is often no visible sign of the exercise of power which gives men control over resources and determines what kinds of behaviour are acceptable and what are not.

3   Marital conflict and high rates of divorce suggest that what kind of order prevails is neither passively accepted nor readily negotiated between partners.

4   The theoretical claim would see conscious agents internalizing the distribution of power within a larger structure, which gives the prevailing order the appearance of being natural and inevitable. Divorce rates suggest more effective powers of agency.

2.8 Consolidating the key tasks

WORKBOOK ACTIVITY 2.11

Finally, we suggest you end your work on Chapter 2 by returning to the list of key tasks at the beginning of this section of the workbook and try to note down a sentence or two about each one. These could well provide a basis for your revision.

3 WORK: FROM CERTAINTY TO FLEXIBILITY?

Chapter 2 concentrated on ways in which power works by ordering people's lives in families. Two kinds of ordering have been implicit in this. The first is concerned with positions in families: for example, the relative powers of men and women. The second is the more commonplace ordering of the routines of everyday life. Two kinds of ordering are also described in Chapter 3. The first is the day-to-day ordering which goes on in any workplace, the second is the ordering undertaken by the market for jobs. The distinction is reflected in different terms: 'work' is the productive activity itself, and 'employment' the distribution of that activity and the contractual arrangements under which it happens. The ordering of lives which takes place through the labour market decides who should work and who should not and who has what income. This is clearly fundamental to understanding how UK society is ordered and what are the relations of power which underlie that ordering.

Like the last chapter, this one traces the transformation in UK society from a 'golden age' of full employment and jobs for life to the contemporary scene which some view as marked by uncertainty and insecurity: a labour market in flexible jobs. Like the last chapter, Chapter 3 does this in three ways, it:

- describes some key social changes,

- looks at how those changes have altered the ways in which society is ordered and power is distributed, and

- considers how political ideologies have shaped change.

The changes Chapter 3 describes are closely associated with the political ideologies of social democracy and liberalism respectively, their social values and the economic theories which helped form them. For social democracy, John Maynard Keynes's theories about full employment are central. For liberalism, those of Freidrich Hayek are used to explain the transformation to flexible work. Alongside these, we continue to draw on the insights of Weber's and Foucault's theories to trace how power might be said to have 'changed sides'. In addition, the chapter introduces Marxist theory and considers its explanations of how power is at work in the changes described. (Incidentally, this is a good point to note that, in social science texts, the term Marx*ist*, in relation to a theory, is usually spelt with a capital M while marx*ism*, the political ideology, often takes a small initial, despite being named after a person. The main reason for this is that the political ideology is understood by many social theorists to have meanings and ideas in its own right which have developed well beyond the writings of Karl Marx himself. In DD100 we have tended to use the capital initial for both, for the sake of simplicity.)

KEY TASKS

Chapter 3, 'Work: From Certainty to Flexibility?'

- Understand what is meant by 'full employment' and how it arose from Keynesian policies.
- Understand the transformation to flexible work and its connection with Hayek's theories.
- Develop an awareness of how labour markets contribute to ordering lives.
- Develop an awareness of how power works through labour markets.
- Make use of different interpretations of power in the labour market following the theories of Marxism, and of Weber and Foucault.
- Examine the key ideas of social democracy, and of liberalism.
- Develop your skills of outlining essay plans for examinations.

Now please read Chapter 3 and then return to this point in the workbook. You should spend about two-thirds of your time working on Chapter 3 and the remaining time on this section of the workbook.

3.1 Uncertainty, diversity and the market in jobs

One of the major arguments that UK society is abandoning old certainties and moving into an uncertain future stems from changes in long-standing patterns in the way work is organized. Flexible working both creates uncertainty and allows diversity, but in what balance?

WORKBOOK ACTIVITY 3.1

Make a list of ways in which changes in employment have affected someone you know, giving particular attention to:

- what kinds of uncertainty were generated by these changes
- any sense in which change results in greater diversity.

Then, using the examples you have given, make a note of what connections you can see between the idea of uncertainty and that of diversity.

COMMENT

No doubt you found a good deal of evidence of uncertainty and some examples of greater diversity as a result of changing employment patterns. We will concentrate on the connections between uncertainty and diversity. We noted three:

1   The changes to flexible working hours and temporary jobs have hugely diversified working patterns, in ways which are more convenient for some and less secure for others.

2   Flexible but insecure working patterns are said to be responses to the diversity of consumer demand and the need for suppliers to offer ever-widening choices to compete.

3   There is greater diversity of ways of organizing working lives which reflect the cultural and ethnic diversification of 'ways of living'.

The old standard ways of organizing work are ceasing to be 'standard'. Increasing diversity and greater uncertainty are *part of the same processes of change*. You will find it useful to keep this connection in mind and to think about causal connections between the two by asking:

● Does the pursuit of greater diversity result in uncertainties?

● Do uncertainties caused by other factors open up scope for greater diversity?

WORKBOOK ACTIVITY 3.2

Look back to your list of anecdotes about work and make notes about:

● The impact of changes on ordering people's lives.

● How power is operating to create ordering.

● Whether you regard the changes as mainly beneficial.

COMMENT

For the first point, we hope you will have considered:

● how the market system divides up jobs

● the organization of working patterns

● what work is open to you and what is not

● the exclusion of some people from work.

The second point might have brought to mind:

● the relative powers of employers and employees

● differences in the power of occupational groups

● inequalities of power between different social groups in the market.

We will return to the question of the benefits of these changes later.

3.2 Questions, claims and evidence: how is work changing?

Section 3 of the chapter brings together evidence to show how flexible working has increased. Following the circuit of knowledge, it begins by *asking* in what ways work in the UK is more flexible than 50 years ago. This then becomes a *claim* that more people work part time, etc., and this is checked against *evidence* of changes in employment in Tables 3.1 and 3.2.

WORKBOOK ACTIVITY 3.3

Look at Tables 3.1 and 3.2 from Chapter 3 (reproduced here as Tables 2 and 3) and note down short answers to each of these questions:

1   Why have categories A–D been included?

2   Why is 'self-employed' included and why is it described as 'without employees'?

3   Why are these years chosen for the table?

4   What do the percentages mean?

5   Which groups of figures should add up to 100 per cent?

6   Why don't they make 100 per cent?

7   Why are there two totals for the proportion in flexible work at the bottom of each column?

TABLE 2   Changes in men's employment, 1975–94

| | Percentages in each category | | | |
	1975	1981	1986	1994
(A) Full-time permanent	n.a.	n.a.	79.3	73.1
(B) Part-time	2.4	1.7	3.5	6.1
(C) Temporary (full-time)	n.a.	n.a.	2.6	3.9
(D) Self-employed without employees	5.8	4.7	9.0	12.4
Flexible (B + D)	8.2	6.4	12.5	18.5
All flexible (B + C + D)	n.a.	n.a.	15.1	22.4

See note below Table 3.

TABLE 3   Changes in women's employment, 1975–94

| | Percentages in each category | | | |
	1975	1981	1986	1994
(A) Full-time permanent	n.a.	n.a.	47.7	46.6
(B) Part-time	39.0	40.6	43.8	43.2
(C) Temporary (full-time)	n.a.	n.a.	1.9	2.8
(D) Self-employed without employees	2.2	1.5	4.5	5.0
Flexible (B + D)	41.2	42.1	48.3	48.2
All flexible (B + C + D)	n.a.	n.a.	50.2	51.0

Note: from the 1950s through to the 1970s the government statisticians who compiled the Labour Force Survey did not feel that it was necessary to distinguish carefully between permanent and temporary full-time employment. Hence the unavailability of the distinction between full-time permanent and full-time temporary employment in the LFS until 1986.

Source: based on Dex and McCulloch, 1995, Tables 4.1 and 4.2; data derived from Labour Force Surveys, 1975–94

COMMENT

Check your answers against ours at the end of the workbook (p.70). If yours differ, look back to the tables and check the reasoning of your answers.

3.3 Assembling a story line: changing power in markets

Woven into Chapter 3 is an important historical story of how power in employment markets has shifted over the last 50 years or so. A useful approach to revision is to 'assemble' parts of a story line into a single piece. Diagrams and time-lines can be a good way of doing this.

Revision skills: assembling a story line

WORKBOOK ACTIVITY 3.4

Look back through Sections 2.1, 2.2, 2.3.2 and 3.2 of Chapter 3 and put together a time-line which summarizes the key features of distinctive phases of employment markets described there.

We suggest you use the following periods:

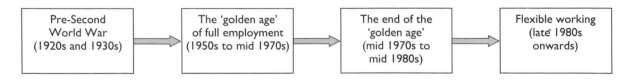

COMMENT _____

Our completed time-line is at the end of the workbook (p.71). Compare yours with ours and note down any points you left out.

WORKBOOK ACTIVITY 3.5

Make notes on which groups were in a powerful position and which a weak position in each period. You could use just *some* of the following distinctions, all of which are used at some point in the chapter to demonstrate differences in power:

- employers and employees
- women and men
- labour and capital
- shareholders and customers
- salaried staff and waged staff
- manual vs. non-manual employees
- different ethnic groups
- different regions.

COMMENT _____

There are a large number of possible points. Here are our brief answers for just one group:

Employers are clearly in stronger positions than employees under flexible working arrangements. Towards the end of the 'golden age' they saw themselves as being in a weaker position, squeezed between powerful unions and overseas competition, when some employees had some real strength in wage bargaining. In the 1930s, employees were in a desperately weak position though some employers were experiencing falling profits. In the early stages of Keynesian demand management relations between the two were more evenly balanced.

End of revision skills

3.4 Summarizing the argument: theorizing changes in power

Chapter 3 introduced the Marxist theory of power to analyse aspects of how power has changed in work and employment. We will now use it to illustrate how theory can help explain the transformation of work and employment, before asking you to do the same for Weber's and Foucault's theories.

Section 2.3.1 looks at how Marxist theory can be used to explain the changes in power which were brought about by the social democratic state. We noted:

- capitalism needs the state to soften edges and avert crises
- the state maintains and justifies inequalities
- full employment meant higher wages, mass consumption and so more profits.

At the end of Section 3.1, which compares Longbridge and Regensberg, the case for flexible hours is theorized. We noted:

- greater flexibility allows firms to make greater profits per worker
- capital can use flexibility to push down wages, since it has more reserves and is more mobile than most workers.

WORKBOOK ACTIVITY 3.6

Now make short notes on the summaries at the end of Sections 3 and 4, and then **summarize the argument** by drawing the notes together into a short general paragraph to answer the question: 'how does a Marxist theory of power explain changes in work?'

Revision skills: summarizing the argument

COMMENT _____

Our paragraph reads as follows:

The Marxist theory of power sees a sharp dividing line between workers and owners, and what is in their respective interests. It views capitalists or owners as generally being in the stronger position. Sometimes, if they are too strong and workers are in a weak position, concessions have to be made to prevent conflicts and crises or to give workers more power to consume, to allow profits to be accumulated. Generally, though, owners are able to keep their advantage over workers as conditions change by:

reducing their dependence on workers by increasing use of technology;

creating competition for jobs;

establishing patterns of flexible working; or

moving their operations to places where labour is cheaper or more flexible.

The fundamental inequalities in power between workers and owners are maintained, as capitalists adapt to different conditions.

WORKBOOK ACTIVITY 3.7

Choosing either Weber's or Foucault's theory of power, look back to the closing paragraphs of Sections 2.3.1, 3.1, 3.2.3 and 4.3, and make very brief notes on what the theory has to say about power. Write a short paragraph on how the theory explains how power operates through the way work and employment are organized.

COMMENT

As a check on your general points, look back to the summaries of these two theories in Section 7, Chapter 1.

End of revision skills

3.5 Marshalling evidence: power and order in the market – liberalism vs. social democracy

Chapter 3 began by asking you about the benefits and drawbacks of flexible employment. Or, to put it another way, do you see flexible employment more in terms of greater uncertainty, or of greater diversity? Questions about what is beneficial or not are, of course, questions about social values.

Social scientists look out for social values in statements, and usually try to break them down into further questions in which the values element can be kept distinctive. The question, 'Is flexible employment beneficial?', gets broken down into:

* Who has benefited from flexible employment?

* According to which social values is that desirable?

Revision skills: marshalling evidence

Let's imagine that the question, 'is flexible employment beneficial?', is an examination question. Think through what **evidence you can marshal** from Chapter 3 to answer it. (This would be a full essay answer, but here we will just outline what you need to cover.)

First, we need evidence on flexible employment.

Part time, solo - self-employed and temporary work is on the increase, but there are more of some kinds for some people.

Second, what might this mean for employees?

Part-time work means a smaller income but can mean multiple incomes.

What of the gains for employers?

The Longbridge/Regensberg example spells out the benefits and so does Hayek's theory of the market.

Who is better off, who is worse off?

Flexible working patterns have created more high earners, but more low earners as well (wage dispersion). Flexible employment may attract poorer rates of pay for some, at least (abolition of wages councils and declining union power). It has also reduced the inequalities between male and female incomes but the difference remains large.

From the employer point of view, flexible working increases profits and competitiveness (Regensberg).

We broke the question down into two questions about benefits and social values – this addresses the first question. For the second question the social values connected with the political ideologies would be a good starting point.

The benefits of flexibility fit well with liberal priorities about individual freedom, the power to choose, greater diversity, minimal state interference and rewards for enterprise.

All these could be developed to say who does well and who does badly.

Social democracy puts forward different values: collective responsibility, state involvement and organized efforts to promote social justice and minimize private misfortune. On this reckoning, the benefits of flexible working are less convincing.

Last of all, sum up and conclude, saying which case you find more persuasive and why.

In effect, we have outlined an essay plan. Notice that the outline is made up of:

- the thread of the argument
- a structure for the essay
- pointers to key elements in the argument
- pointers to evidence which will be used.

But what it does not try to do is to:

- spell out the arguments in full
- elaborate on the main points to be made about particular views
- describe in detail what a particular theory or viewpoint says
- include detailed evidence about statistics, policies, historical events, etc.

WORKBOOK ACTIVITY 3.8

Construct an outline plan for a full essay in answer to the question:

Why does liberalism regard flexible employment as of benefit to all?

In this question you are being asked to concentrate in a bit more depth on just one aspect of what we covered in answering 'is flexible employment beneficial?' (immediately above). Much of the same information will be relevant, but with different emphasis and a different line of argument.

COMMENT

End of revision skills

If you got into difficulties with this, check back to the list of what to include and what to exclude.

3.6 Consolidating the key tasks

WORKBOOK ACTIVITY 3.9

Finally, we suggest once again that you round off your work this week by going back to the list of key tasks with which this section of the workbook began and try writing a sentence or two about each of them. As a further step towards practising the kinds of short summary exam-type answers you will meet in TMA 03, take the task on the list you found it easiest to write about and build your sentences up into a short paragraph, writing for no more than 15 minutes.

4 WELFARE: FROM SECURITY TO RESPONSIBILITY?

The final chapter of Book 3 looks at the public institutions which have direct involvement in ordering people's lives: those of state welfare. Through them the state has far-reaching influence over the way we live. State welfare has been the focus of major political struggles in the modern UK, most of which have been identified with political ideologies, inspired by the exceptional opportunities which state welfare presents to shape UK society *by means of* ordering lives. The influence of social democracy and of liberalism in particular are explained, and feminist and Marxist critiques are also addressed.

Chapter 4 focuses on two key periods in the recent history of the welfare state: the so-called 'golden age' of post-Second World War welfare and the restructuring of welfare in the 1980s and 1990s. Both periods represent transformations in the distribution of power, and the theories of Weber and Foucault are used to assess these transformations.

KEY TASKS

Chapter 4, 'Welfare: From Security to Responsibility?'

- Understand the transformations which lead to the social democratic welfare state and the transformations which lead to its restructuring.

- Look at the ways in which institutions of welfare order lives.

- Consider how the ordering processes of welfare entail the exercise of power.

- Understand how the theories of Weber and of Foucault make sense of the processes of ordering.

- Examine the key role of the political ideology of social democracy in shaping the post-war welfare state.

- Understand the key role of liberalism as a political ideology in restructuring welfare in the 1980s and 1990s.

- Be aware of the critiques of state welfare put forward by Marxism and by feminism.

- Develop your skills of planning and practising exam answers.

Now please read Chapter 4, 'Welfare: From Security to Responsibility?' and return to this point in the workbook. You should spend around two-thirds of your time on Chapter 4 and the remainder on this section of the workbook.

4.1 Theorizing order in welfare institutions

We would like you to build on Activities 4.1 and 4.2 in Chapter 4, to think more about your experiences of welfare institutions, and how they can be theorized.

WORKBOOK ACTIVITY 4.1

Complete the following grid, based on experiences you have had of welfare institutions in recent years, one positive, one negative. You should indicate the key features of the experience, then note down how lives become ordered through it. Finally, how do Weber's and Foucault's theories of power interpret the experience?

Experience	How it orders lives	Weberian interpretation	Foucauldian interpretation
1			
2			

COMMENT _____

We suggest that you use Table 1.1 in Chapter 1 to check whether you have represented the two theories of power accurately and applied them fairly. If you can't see much connection between what you have written in the 'interpretation' boxes, treat this as a good opportunity to work out what has gone wrong.

_____

4.2 Writing practice answers: Weber and social democracy – theory and political ideology (again)

In this section, we want to trace the connections between Weber's theories about power, the state and social class, and social democracy, as the political ideology which shaped the post-war welfare state. At the same time you will be able to improve your examination answer technique of writing succinct summaries by **writing practice answers**.

Revision skills: writing practice answers

To begin with, it would be useful to consolidate what you have learned about Weber so far in DD100.

WORKBOOK ACTIVITY 4.2

Write a short summary of about 150 words saying what you think is meant by this quote from Chapter 4, Section 2.2:

> ... the state is seen as holding the balance of power between competing interests – social classes for example – on the basis of its own rationality.

To do so, you should go back and read:

  Book 1, Chapter 3, Section 5, especially Section 5.3.

  Book 3, Chapter 1, Section 5.

  Book 3, Chapter 4, Section 2.2.

Following the techniques of *extracting*, *processing* and *re-presenting* from the *Introductory Workbook*, highlight the critical concepts, make notes on each one, then put them together in summary form.

COMMENT _____

First, we highlighted the following concepts:

  the state

  balance of power

competing interests

social classes

rationality

Next we made notes about each one. For example, our notes about social classes read as follows:

Weber's theory of social class sees a number of distinct classes competing for positions. A large part of this is about positions based on people's places in the occupational hierarchy, or success in the labour market. But there are many divisions between classes not solely based upon wealth and income. Differences in status and power also distinguish separate classes.

Finally we connected up our notes, and edited them down to the bare essentials to produce the following summary:

According to Weber, societies consist of competing interests which try to gain advantage. Most important are differing social classes, whose members compete to secure good jobs and positions of influence. The task of the state is to ensure that this competition occurs with minimal conflict and social disorder. This means seeing that it is done fairly by reference to widely understood rules. For example, it would be up to the state to see that there were ways of resolving disputes. The state holds the balance of power through institutions like arbitration bodies and courts of law in which people who are given power in an official capacity by the state decide what is fair, using a rational system of laws or procedures to resolve conflicts, impartially and impersonally.

This is very much how the state is also seen by social democracy: the neutral arbiter carrying out the wishes of democratically elected governments. So theories influence the reasoning of a political ideology. This is visible in the way the social democratic welfare state was set up. It was devoted to constructing forms of welfare provision, as part of its work of ordering.

End of revision skills

WORKBOOK ACTIVITY 4.3

Skim read Section 2 of Chapter 4 to pick out aspects of the social democratic welfare state which fit in with this Weberian conception. Make brief notes which illustrate the connection between the political ideology and Weber's theories. This will consolidate your revision technique of **actively searching for relevant material**.

Revision skills: actively searching for relevant material

C O M M E N T

We went through just the first few paragraphs of Section 2 and made the following notes.

- The state is democratically empowered to pursue equal rights and social justice.
- State institutions should be above political interference.
- Political parties, business, trade unions have competing interests.
- State institutions balance those interests.
- State institutions make fair decisions based on professional knowledge.

There is much more in the remaining paragraphs which illustrate the connection further, which we hope you have covered.

End of revision skills

4.3 Political ideologies, social science methods and social values

The connections between social science and political ideology do not end with the influence of theories. As we saw in the chapter, the thinking underlying some ideologies draws directly on social science methods. Social democracy envisaged forms of rational activity and informed judgement which aimed to turn decision making about how to order lives and make reforms into a social *science*, unfolding its own impartial reasoning.

WORKBOOK ACTIVITY 4.4

Using the circuit of knowledge, think through how social science might help to steer social democratic reforms, in relation to *one* of:

- child poverty,
- universal medical treatment, or
- family breakdown.

Begin by constructing a *question*, then derive a *claim* from it, then suggest what *evidence* would be needed.

COMMENT

For child poverty our version looks like this:

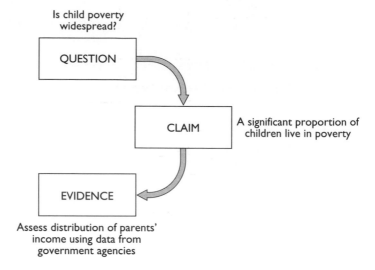

No doubt you have come up with different questions, claims and evidence. To check yours, see whether there is a clear reasoned connection between the question and the claim, and between the claim and the evidence to be sought.

For social scientists there is always a question of what underlies the reasoning that has been adopted. To take the example of child poverty, our question leans towards the possibility that poverty exists amongst children. A social scientist influenced by liberalism might ask a more sceptical question ('is there any reason to believe that child poverty is at unacceptable levels?'), and use a different definition of poverty. Here the values of the ideology are pulling the question in a different direction. Or, in the case of the evidence to be sought, feminists argue that our evidence cannot provide a sound assessment of the claim because how resources are used to benefit children depends on the degree of control women have over family income, and that much female poverty is invisible to government agencies. Here the theories and the social values of feminism query whether the evidence is well matched to the claim.

So the 'golden age' view from within social democracy that neutral, impartial and scientific methods can provide rational solutions to social problems comes into question. Social values and theories are important features of the circuit of knowledge as our 'enhanced' diagram shows (Figure 4).

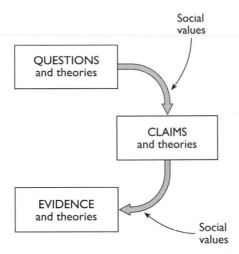

FIGURE 4 Social values in the circuit of knowledge

Look again at *your* responses to the last activity. Can you detect value assumptions at work in the connections between question, claim and evidence? Are they associated with any political ideology? Is a particular theory informing the reasoning? Try to be explicit about these, following the approach we took regarding child poverty.

C O M M E N T _____

The answer to all these questions must be 'yes'. We hope you have been able to see the specific influences they may have exerted.

Recognizing that social science methods and the circuit of knowledge all inescapably entail the influence of social values and the work of theories is not to be critical of them, or imply that they cannot deliver the promise of 'scientific knowledge'. It is simply to recognize that all such knowledge has to be interpreted as being a social product which has arisen out of a particular set of values and understandings.

4.4 Marxism: theory and ideology

Earlier, we looked at the multi-faceted nature of feminism as a political ideology, a distinctive set of theories and a social movement. This is not unique to feminism. Indeed, you may already have noticed that Marxism was introduced in Chapter 3 as a way of *theorizing* about how power shifted in work and employment. It offered an important contrast to Weber's and Foucault's theories by placing strong emphasis on *structures* of power and their imperviousness to change. In Chapter 4, though, Marxism was presented as a political ideology – in this instance as a critique of the social democratic conception of the welfare state. And Marxism has, of course, also been a movement for revolutionary change.

As we have seen, theories and political ideologies are not the same. Theories are reasoned-out explanations of the world as it is now, political ideologies are coherent collections of ideas, beliefs and social values about the world as their proponents think it should be. But we have also seen that ideologies draw on theories – as in the case of social democracy and Keynes's theories, and liberalism and Hayek's. Marxism provides a good opportunity to look briefly at how the two can connect.

WORKBOOK ACTIVITY 4.6

Look back to the summary in Section 3.4, Workbook Activity 3.6 of the Marxist theory of power as it applies to work. Then look carefully through the points listed under Marxism on the political ideologies grid at the end of Chapter 4 (Table 4.3).

Identify two or three points where you can see the connections between theory and political ideology which illustrate the 'world as it is/world as it should be' distinction.

C O M M E N T _____

We offer two examples below. There are many others, which we hope you will find.

Inequality

Theory: capitalists are in a position of great strength over workers.

Political ideology: social values are centred on creating social equality.

Welfare

Theory: welfare concessions are offered when the inequalities of capitalism are so great as to threaten stability and the social order.

Political ideology: the state is the tool of capitalism, always acting in the interests of the dominant class and must, therefore, be overthrown if social equality is to be achieved.

_____

In both cases, the theoretical statement offers a reasoned explanation of the world as it is; the political ideology indicates what should be. It is clear that the theory informs the political ideology. But the theory has an existence in its own right and makes sense without the ideology. Political ideology can stand without theory but is greatly strengthened by it. Also, as we saw in the previous section (Section 4.3), the kinds of values on which ideologies are built do also affect what questions get asked in the first place and how they are translated into claims and the search for evidence. So there is an important but very variable and sometimes complex two-way relationship between theories and political ideologies, which we can represent as:

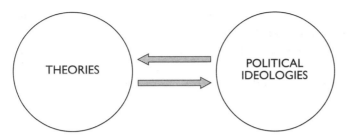

4.5 Re-working lists and grids: comparing political ideologies

In Section 3.5 (above), we began to make some comparisons between liberalism and social democracy. Comparing two perspectives like this is something you are often asked to do for an examination. The next activity is intended to get you started on that but also to help you develop another exam revision technique: **re-working lists/grids into a plan and then an essay.**

So far we have used grids as a way of summarizing key points into a clear framework. We can now use a grid as an aid to memory to do a specific task.

Revision skills: re-working lists/grids into an essay

WORKBOOK ACTIVITY 4.7

Using the grid in Table 4.3 at the end of Chapter 4, put together a plan for answering the following question, which is the sort of question you might be asked in TMA 03:

> Compare the social democratic and liberal views of how the welfare state should exert power over people's lives.

We suggest that you approach this as follows, and then practise writing a full essay answer, allowing yourself about 45 minutes.

- Think carefully through the list of points under the 'power and ordering lives' heading for social democracy and then do the same for liberalism.
- Pick one point from social democracy which seems to show a significant point of difference from liberalism.
- Write out in prose form what the difference is.

- Say briefly how the difference arises (the 'social values' column might be useful here).

- Give an example of how this might show up (the 'institutions and structures' column might help here).

- Then move on to another pair of points of contrast and do the same.

C O M M E N T _____

Here is our attempt, using the grid for just one point of contrast.

Social democracy looks to the institutions of the welfare state to secure the welfare of citizens. For liberals, this is much more a matter for the individual and individual agency – that is, the power of the individual to make arrangements for their own security and welfare. The contrast is essentially one about structures (advocated by social democracy) and agency (favoured by liberalism). Much of this contrast can be traced to the social values of the two political ideologies. For social democracy, all citizens should have equal rights to basic forms of welfare so that they have equal opportunities to prosper. For liberals, welfare is an infringement of individual freedom but also takes away personal responsibility. An example of how these differences can be seen is where social democrats call for higher taxation to fund state welfare, while liberals encourage the individual to make private insurance arrangements for health, unemployment, etc.

In 45 minutes you might expect to write three or four such paragraphs, plus an introduction and conclusion.

End of revision skills

_____

Try to practise other comparisons like this. You can take any pair of political ideologies and compare them on social values, institutions and structures, or power and ordering. Particularly useful to work on would be:

- liberalism and social democracy on institutions and structures

- Marxism and social democracy on power and ordering

- feminism and liberalism on social values.

Make up your own question based on these comparisons.

4.6 'Client-citizens' and consumers: changing power?

To bring your work on Chapter 4 to a close we suggest that you compare the old conception of welfare users as 'client-citizens' with the changed conception of them as welfare consumers, using the theories of Weber and

Foucault to interpret them. This is the most challenging task we have set in this workbook and you should not feel dispirited if you can only manage a very basic version of it. Even that will be a useful consolidation of your work.

WORKBOOK ACTIVITY 4.8

Re-read Section 2.2 (especially Section 2.2.3) and Section 4.3 (especially the sub-section entitled 'From citizens and clients to consumers'), making notes on the main distinctions between the old conception of welfare users as 'client-citizens' with the changed conception of them as welfare consumers. Then read ahead in each sub-section to the material on how the Weberian theory of power makes sense of each one. Picking just one aspect of each, jot down one or two phrases about the difference, if any, between the two when seen through Weber's theory. (If you are stuck, read our short account below and then try to do the same on another aspect of it.)

COMMENT _____

We concentrated on the relationship between professionals and welfare users, and made the following notes:

Under the old views of users as 'client-citizens' this is relatively straightforward, as understood in Weberian terms. They are passive recipients of welfare from professionals whose expertise and specialist knowledge confers an authority which the user has no choice but to accept. This might be a doctor, a social worker, a teacher, etc. The recipient is seen as dependent upon the activity of the professional, without whose help they would be in difficulties and whose expertise they are bound to accept.

(We would sum this up as: passive recipients; dependent upon experts.)

What has occurred following the transformation of welfare is that 'client-citizens' are now constructed as consumers. To the extent that this affects the relationship of power between them and professionals, they have some new rights to ask for explanations of the attention they are receiving and perhaps to seek alternatives. In this sense the professional is made partially accountable for his or her actions. However, Weber's theory would argue that the basis of the old powers and authority is largely unchanged in practice, and remains rooted deep in the structures built around expertise and specialist knowledge.

(We would sum this up as: underlying structures of power unaltered; professional power more accountable but not reduced.)

WORKBOOK ACTIVITY 4.9

Now repeat the exercise making notes on how Foucault's theory would see power here. (Again, if you are finding this difficult, read our version and then try your own on another aspect of the changes.)

COMMENT

Our notes are as follows:

Here the passivity of dependent clients would be explained in terms of norms and expectations of the user-professional relationship based on historical practice. There is neither the imagination, the language, nor the channels to do things differently. All the parties involved subscribe to this way of making the user-professional relationship.

(We would sum this up as: norms not rules of passivity; absence of means to ask or challenge experts.)

When users become talked of as welfare consumers the very fact of naming them in this way raises comparison with shoppers and their powers to choose and challenge. This gives the new welfare consumer a legitimate voice and allows proper challenge to the authority of providers. In other words, the consumer is ascribed a degree of agency not envisaged for the 'client-citizen'.

(We would sum this up as: possibilities for agency through legitimate consumer voice; professional authority challengable.)

We cannot guess at all the aspects of this activity you might have covered. However, the grid at the end of this workbook (p.72) gives a very brief summary of the points we have made and some other examples. It is no more than a guide, and is certainly not 'an answer' to be learned by rote for TMA 03. The important part of the activity is 'reasoning out' your summary.

4.7 Consolidating the key tasks

WORKBOOK ACTIVITY 4.10

Finally, we recommend that, even if you have not done so at the end of the previous sections, you should return to the list of key tasks with which this section began. Either try writing a sentence or two about as many of the tasks as you can, or, if you are feeling more confident, choose two tasks from the list and spend 10–15 minutes writing a paragraph about each of them.

5 REFLECTION AND CONSOLIDATION

You have now reached the end of your work on the individual chapters of Block 3. The final work for this block is to enable you to think about the block as a whole, reflect on what it has raised and consolidate what you have learned. So far we have looked at changes in the family, in work and in welfare as though they were three separate institutions. But, of course, change in one frequently has important impacts on changes in the other. Some of these have been mentioned already – the impact of changes at work on the family, for example, or the pressures which the transformations in work placed on the welfare state. But there are other important connections. Think, for example, of the simultaneous influence of liberalism in the transformations in employment and in welfare. There are many more such connections which we will not have time to cover, but the Afterword to Book 3 and Side B of Audio-cassette 5 both draw together some of them. They will help greatly with consolidating your work and preparing for TMA 03.

 Pause now to read the Afterword to Book 3, then listen to Side B of Audio-cassette 5 immediately afterwards and read the notes on it. You should also try to watch (depending on broadcast schedules) TV 03 around now and read the notes on it. Then return to this point and consolidate your reading and listening with Workbook Activity 5.1.

WORKBOOK ACTIVITY 5.1

Make some brief notes under the following headings:

- connections between changes in the family and work
- connections between changes in the family and welfare
- connections between changes in work and welfare.

5.1 Uncertainty and diversity, structure and agency, power and ordering

Another useful way of reflecting on your work on Block 3 is, as ever, to use the DD100 themes, plus the Block 3 theme of *power and ordering*. These themes may be the subject of the questions in TMA 03. We therefore suggest you work carefully through the following activity.

WORKBOOK ACTIVITY 5.2

Complete the following grid, making short notes of key issues and ideas. We have completed one entry for each cell to get you started. Try to enter at least one or two more points in most cells. If you are stuck, look back through the relevant workbook section for each chapter (*including* Chapter 1). You will find at least one section of your work related to the relevant theme. In many cases it will be the subject of a whole sub-section.

	Uncertainty and diversity	Structure and agency	Power and ordering
Families	Changes in male/ female relations in families.	Men in structurally stronger positions in traditional family.	Lives ordered by authority or by habit and custom?

	Uncertainty and diversity	Structure and agency	Power and ordering
Work and employment	Loss of 'jobs for life' widens possibilities for some.	Active agents free to create own openings in free market.	Free market increases wage differentials.
Welfare	Slimmed down welfare reduces sense of security for some.	Old welfare structures enforce fair distribution of state resources.	Institutions and professionals shape people's daily lives.

5.2 Theories and the circuit of knowledge

The other important element of Block 3 is the skill of recognizing and using theories, the influence of social values and the place of both in the circuit of knowledge. At this stage we are not asking you to do any special work in pulling these together because the circuit of knowledge is an important feature of the *Mid Course Review* which follows. If you are able to bring any of these points and the significance of the enhanced circuit of knowledge diagram on page 29 into your TMA 03 answer, your tutor-counsellor will give you credit for it.

5.3 Family, work and welfare: reading the future

Block 3 was written in 1999 and, as the conclusion to Chapter 4 and the Afterword to Book 3 make clear, there are further efforts to bring about other important changes in the area of welfare in particular, but also in family policy and employment. To get the most from this block you might find it useful and stimulating to watch the changes in these institutions. One of the benefits of understanding political ideologies is that they provide a lasting framework which can help you to make sense of the wider set of ideas which lie behind policies. *If you have time*, we suggest that you find one newspaper article about changes in the family, one on employment, and one on welfare, make notes on the key aspects of policy which are changing and see how far you can link them to the political ideologies. There will be plenty of scope for finding policies which have their roots in liberalism or in social democracy in particular, but the others remain highly influential. New policies will not always match a single ideology well and many policies are hybrids and compromises between competing political factions, but the underlying ideologies are often clearly visible.

6 REVISION SKILLS AND ASSESSING BLOCK 3

For the week before you complete TMA 03, we would like you to do some more work on Block 3 as though you were revising for a conventional examination. The remainder of this workbook is intended to guide your preparation and to give you some advice on exam technique which will stand you in good stead for future conventional exams. Of course, you have already been doing a lot of this as you studied this workbook. Here, all we ask you to do is to apply the revision advice we have already given you, on the following skills:

- active revision (Section 1.4)

- searching for relevant material (Section 2.2)

- assembling a story line (Section 3.3)

- summarizing the argument (Section 3.4)

- marshalling evidence (Section 3.5)

- writing practice answers (Section 4.2)

- actively searching for relevant material (Section 4.2)

- re-working lists/grids into an essay (Section 4.5).

For each of these, we suggest you look back to the relevant section, then, taking one of the questions in the *Assignments Booklet* for TMA 03, decide how you can practise answering it.

Use the preparation week to:

- Look back over the block as a whole.

- Use the Introduction and Afterword to Book 3 to focus on the main concepts, themes, and theories running through it.

- Find connections between the four chapters of the book using the course themes.

- Begin to think about the circuit of knowledge.

- Develop techniques for answering the TMA 03 questions.

 Pause now and read carefully through the *Assignments Booklet*, but please note that you need to complete your work on Section 6 before you attempt TMA 03. So return to this point when you have read the *Assignments Booklet*.

6.1 General tips on completing TMA 03 (also relevant for future exams)

Our biggest single tip is: be sure to complete TMA 03 in your study centre if you possibly can. It will be tempting to do it in the privacy of your own home, without your tutor-counsellor watching or other students around you. But this will give you very little of the 'feel' of doing a real exam and, when you come to next year's course, the compulsory exam will feel like an alien experience. You don't have to pass TMA 03 to pass DD100, so take the chance. The more nervous you feel about completing TMA 03 in your study centre, the more likely it is that the experience will help you for next year's course exams.

The following points are widely regarded as good exam technique:

1 Timing

Before you begin, be absolutely clear how long you should spend on each answer. This should be a direct reflection of the proportion of marks given for each answer. In TMA 03, the timings shown do this and you should make every effort to stick to them.

2 Answer the question

Make sure you read the question carefully two or three times, underline key words and phrases and be quite clear in your own mind what the examiner is looking for. At all costs, make sure you ANSWER THE QUESTION. Don't translate it into another question which you are more confident about answering. Avoid writing down everything you know about the topic without applying it to the question. Only include relevant material.

3 Make a plan

It can be a good idea to spend a few minutes quickly scribbling out key terms, concepts, facts, theories and so on to provide a resource you can return to as you write. But more important than this is to plan. You won't have time to write an outline, but a plan of a few headings is essential, otherwise your answer risks losing structure and direction.

4 Pause for thought

It is very easy to feel so relieved that you have something to say that you go off in your own direction and lose sight of the question or the time. Try to get into the habit of making yourself pause every 10–15 minutes to do three things:

- re-read the question and make sure you are moving towards an answer to this question (not another one),
- look back to your plan (and your list of key ideas, etc.) to see that you have not wandered off, and
- remind yourself of how much time you have left.

5   Helping the assessor to see the point

Try to get into the habit of thinking of the person who will assess your work as someone studying social sciences at the same level as you but at another university. You can assume that they will have a grasp of basic social science ideas but won't necessarily be studying the same things as you are. This should help you to do the following, all of which help to make clear what you are saying and why:

- say at the beginning what you plan to do
- at the end of each major paragraph or section say what it contributes to the argument
- provide signposts which say where you are going next
- explain what you mean by important concepts
- be prepared to state the obvious
- use the penultimate paragraph to summarize the gist of your argument
- be sure to write a conclusion which is closely focused on the question.

These points apply primarily to full-length essays (see also *Workbook 2*, Section 7.4).

6   Facts, names and figures

TMA 03 and examinations are a chance for you to show understanding of ideas, theories, arguments and some of the complex relationships between them. They are not tests of memory. Facts, names and even figures can be useful in giving supporting evidence to substantiate an argument or query a theory. But use them sparingly and only for this purpose. There is no credit for reproducing information which does not contribute directly to an argument.

7   If you run out of time

Write answers in note form rather than leave them incomplete. Even a list of concepts, names and theories can gain you a few marks.

6.2 What to do when TMA 03 comes back

When you get TMA 03 back, it's worth returning to the ten tips which were given at the end of the *Introductory Workbook* (Section 8.5). The main reason for having TMA 03 rather than an exam is so that you can see what you did well, understand where things went wrong, and improve your technique. Your tutor-counsellor's comments will do most of this for you. But only you can take them in and translate them into lessons for your first real exam. If you can, make a list of instructions to yourself for next year as a reminder of where you are vulnerable. This might include comments like:

- relate the answer more explicitly to the question
- show more evidence of knowledge of course materials

- spell out what you understand by key concepts and theories
- remember to write a conclusion
- spell out the relevance of factual information to the argument
- give more time to planning the answer
- be careful not to spend a disproportionate time on early questions
- practise structuring answers during revision
- use more/less detail to back up your points.

When you have completed TMA 03 and done this follow-up work, you will be safely past the half-way mark of DD100. So perhaps this is a good time to congratulate yourself, and remember that even responsible self-governing agents give themselves days off!

In week 20 your guide is the *Mid Course Review*. This is something of a 'pause for thought' week in which we will ask you to look back over the work you have done in the Introductory Block and Blocks 1–3, pull out the connections and the way arguments are building up, and think about the course themes – especially the knowledge and knowing theme – and the circuit of knowledge. These tasks are focused around issues of race and ethnicity some of which have been emerging in the material so far.

COMMENT ON WORKBOOK
ACTIVITY 1.5 _____

Agency	
Weber	Agents exercise power Agents' power comes from positions in organizations
Foucault	Power works on and through agents Anonymous forces (ideas, expectations) work on agents By working with these forces agents themselves exercise power

COMMENT ON WORKBOOK
ACTIVITY 1.6 _____

Structure	
Weber	Structures determine the powers of agents Structure disperses power and gives top-down control Individuals as agents are heavily constrained by structures
Foucault	Structures constrain people by closing down other possibilities Structures are produced by powerful agents negotiating power Complex and changing networks as much as fixed structures shape power

C O M M E N T   O N   W O R K B O O K
A C T I V I T Y   1.8

Weber	Foucault
<u>Who</u> holds power?	<u>How</u> does power work?
Where power <u>is</u>	Where power <u>circulates</u>
Power exercised through chains of command	Power is negotiated through acts of provocation
Power is exercised <u>through</u> agents	Power is taken <u>by</u> agents
Externalized controls	Internalized discipline
Visible hierarchies of power	Shifting networks of power

C O M M E N T   O N   W O R K B O O K
A C T I V I T Y   3.3

1 Why have categories A–D been included?

Because there are three different kinds of 'flexible' working for which data are collected.

2 Why is 'self-employed' included and why is it described as 'without employees'?

People running their own business single-handed may be as likely as an employee on a temporary contract to be without a job or an income.

3 Why are these years chosen for the table?

These are the most recent data (at the time of writing), and it shows the change at (roughly) equal intervals, to make the comparisons in the rate of change valid.

4 What do the percentages mean?

In 1986 79.3 per cent of men who worked did so full time, compared to 3.5 per cent who did so part time and so on.

5 Which groups of figures should add up to 100 per cent?

The total for A, B, C and D.

6 Why don't they make 100 per cent?

The short answer is because the data in the table are incomplete. For 1975 and 1981, the data are incomplete because the government did not differentiate between temporary and permanent full-time employment. For the other two years other figures (people on training schemes and self-employed with employees) have been left out because they are not relevant.

7 Why are there two totals for the proportion in flexible work at the bottom of each column?

This is to compensate for the missing data in 1975 and 1981. It allows us to see the longer-term trend (1975–94) for two 'flexible' categories; but it shows a fuller total for the shorter period (1986–94) for the more comprehensive total which includes temporary full-time employees.

C O M M E N T   O N   W O R K B O O K
A C T I V I T Y   3.4 _____

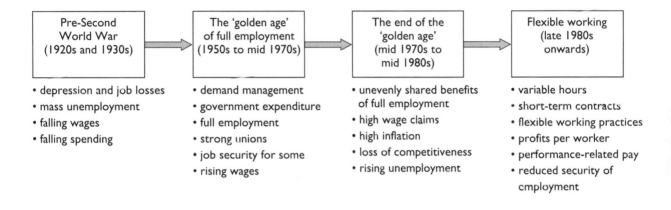

Pre-Second World War (1920s and 1930s)	The 'golden age' of full employment (1950s to mid 1970s)	The end of the 'golden age' (mid 1970s to mid 1980s)	Flexible working (late 1980s onwards)
• depression and job losses • mass unemployment • falling wages • falling spending	• demand management • government expenditure • full employment • strong unions • job security for some • rising wages	• unevenly shared benefits of full employment • high wage claims • high inflation • loss of competitiveness • rising unemployment	• variable hours • short-term contracts • flexible working practices • profits per worker • performance-related pay • reduced security of employment

COMMENT ON WORKBOOK ACTIVITIES 4.8 AND 4.9

	'Client-citizen'	Consumer
Weber	Passive recipient	Underlying structures of power largely unaffected by changes
	Dependent upon professionals	Professionals more accountable but not less powerful
	Exercise of rights/duties	Only some can exploit new opportunities
	Bureaucratic/rational allocation of resources	Old inequalities magnified by markets in welfare
Foucault	Norms not rules cause of passivity	Voice of consumer made legitimate
	Language and channels to ask or challenge not developed	Professional authority can be challenged
	Bureaucratic processes quietly subverted/ignored	Exercise of choice but from prescribed options
	Excluded groups found spaces to intervene and challenge	New norms of individual responsibility internalized

REFERENCES

Dex, S. and McCulloch, A. (1995) *Flexible Employment in Britain: A Statistical Analysis*, Manchester, Equal Opportunities Commission.

Social Trends, London, HMSO (annual).

ACKNOWLEDGEMENTS

Grateful acknowledgement is made to the following sources for permission to reproduce material in this workbook.

Tables

Table 1: Office for National Statistics (1999) *Social Trends*, no.29, © Crown copyright is reproduced with the permission of the Controller of Her Majesty's Stationery Office; Tables 2 and 3: adapted from Dex, S. and McCulloch, A. (1995) *Flexible Employment in Britain: A Statistical Analysis, Research Discussion Series No.15*, Equal Opportunities Commission/*Labour Force Surveys*, Office for National Statistics, © Crown copyright is reproduced with the permission of the Controller of Her Majesty's Stationery Office.

Cover

Image copyright © 1996 PhotoDisc, Inc.

STUDY SKILLS INDEX

revision, searching for relevant material, 29, 52 (WB3)
revision, writing practice answers, 51 (WB3)

scan, 17 (IWB)
searching for relevant material, 29, 52 (WB3)
self-evaluation questions, 53 (IWB)
self-help groups, 13 (IWB)
self-help groups, use of, 62 (WB1)
signposting words, 56 (WB1); 89 (WB2)
skim, 17 (IWB)
social values in the circuit of knowledge, 29, 34, 55 (WB3)
students, support from, 13 (IWB)
students with disabilities, special support, 63 (WB1)
study problems, coping with, 81 (WB2)
studying, strengths and weaknesses, 81 (WB2)

tabular notes, 31 (IWB)
telephone, use of, 62 (WB1)
telephoning your tutor, ground rules, 63 (WB1)
theories, 12 (WB1)
theories in the circuit of knowledge, 10, 64 (WB3)
theories, recognizing and using, 10 (WB3)
TMA 03, reflecting on, 67 (WB3)
TMA 03, tips on completing, 66 (WB3)
tutorials, use of, 62 (WB1)
tutors, support from, 12 (IWB)

writing practice answers, 51 (WB3)
writing skills, 14 (WB1)
writing skills, reflecting on your TMAs, 60 (WB2)
writing skills, structuring your argument, 49 (WB2)